The survey kit

# THE SURVEY KIT

**Purpose.** The purposes of this 9-volume Kit are to enable readers to prepare and conduct surveys and become better users of survey results. Surveys are conducted to collect information by asking questions of people on the telephone, face-to-face, and by mail. The questions can be about attitudes, beliefs, and behavior as well as socioeconomic and health status. To do a good survey also means knowing how to ask questions, design the survey (research) project, sample respondents, collect reliable and valid information, and analyze and report the results. You also need to know how to plan and budget for your survey.

**Users.** The Kit is for students in undergraduate and graduate classes in the social and health sciences and for individuals in the public and private sectors who are responsible for conducting and using surveys. Its primary goal is to enable users to prepare surveys and collect data that are accurate and useful for primarily practical purposes. Sometimes, these practical purposes overlap the objectives of scientific research, and so survey researchers will also find the Kit useful.

**Format of the Kit.** All books in the series contain instructional objectives, exercises and answers, examples of surveys in use and illustrations of survey questions, guidelines for action, checklists of do's and don'ts, and annotated references.

### Volumes in the Survey Kit:

1. **The Survey Handbook**
   *Arlene Fink*

2. **How to Ask Survey Questions**
   *Arlene Fink*

3. **How to Conduct Self-Administered and Mail Surveys**
   *Linda B. Bourque* and *Eve P. Fielder*

4. **How to Conduct Interviews by Telephone and in Person**
   *James H. Frey* and *Sabine Mertens Oishi*

5. **How to Design Surveys**
   *Arlene Fink*

6. **How to Sample in Surveys**
   *Arlene Fink*

7. **How to Measure Survey Reliability and Validity**
   *Mark S. Litwin*

8. **How to Analyze Survey Data**
   *Arlene Fink*

9. **How to Report on Surveys**
   *Arlene Fink*

THE SURVEY KIT

TSK 6

# HOW TO
# SAMPLE
# IN SURVEYS

## ARLENE FINK

**SAGE Publications**
*International Educational and Professional Publisher*
Thousand Oaks   London   New Delhi

For information address:

SAGE Publications, Inc.
2455 Teller Road
Thousand Oaks, California 91320
E-mail: order@sagepub.com

SAGE Publications Ltd.
6 Bonhill Street
London EC2A 4PU
United Kingdom

SAGE Publications India Pvt. Ltd.
M-32 Market
Greater Kailash I
New Delhi 110 048 India

Printed in the United States of America

Library of Congress Cataloging-in-Publication Data

Main entry under title:

The survey kit.
    p.  cm.
   Includes bibliographical references.
   Contents: v. 1. The survey handbook / Arlene Fink — v. 2. How to ask survey questions / Arlene Fink — v. 3. How to conduct self-administered and mail surveys / Linda B. Bourque, Eve P. Fielder — v. 4. How to conduct interviews by telephone and in person / James H. Frey, Sabine Mertens Oishi — v. 5. How to design surveys / Arlene Fink — v. 6. How to sample in surveys / Arlene Fink — v. 7. How to measure survey reliability and validity / Mark S. Litwin — v. 8. How to analyze survey data / Arlene Fink — v. 9. How to report on surveys / Arlene Fink.
   ISBN 0-8039-7388-8 (pbk. : The survey kit : alk. paper)
   1. Social surveys.  2. Health surveys.  I. Fink, Arlene.
HN29.S724   1995
300'.723—dc20                                  95-12712

Sage Production Editor:  Diane S. Foster
Sage Copy Editor:  Joyce Kuhn
Sage Typesetter:  Janelle LeMaster

# Contents

# How to Sample in Surveys:
## Learning Objectives

The aim of this book is to guide the reader in selecting and using appropriate sampling methods. The following specific objectives are stated in terms of aspirations for the reader.

- Distinguish between target populations and samples:

  - Identify research questions and survey objectives
  - Specify inclusion and exclusion criteria

- Choose the appropriate probability and nonprobability sampling methods:

  - Simple random sampling
  - Stratified random sampling
  - Systematic sampling
  - Cluster sampling
  - Convenience sampling
  - Snowball sampling
  - Quota sampling
  - Focus groups

- Understand the logic in estimating standard errors

- Understand the logic in sample size determinations

- Understand the sources of error in sampling

- Calculate the response rate

# 1

# Target Populations and Samples

A sample is a portion or subset of a larger group called a population. The population is the universe to be sampled. Sample populations might include all Americans, residents of California during the 1994 earthquake, and all people over 85 years of age. Surveys often use samples rather than populations.

A good sample is a miniature version of the population—just like it, only smaller. The best sample is **representative,** or a model, of the population. A sample is representative of the population if important characteristics (e.g., age, gender, health status) are distributed similarly in both groups. Suppose the population of interest consists of 1,000 people, 50% of whom are male, with 45% over 65 years of age. A representative sample will have fewer people, say, 500, but it must also consist of 50% males, with 45% over the age of 65.

Survey samples are not meaningful in themselves. Their importance lies in the accuracy with which they represent or mirror the target population. The target population consists of the institutions, persons, problems, and systems to which or whom the survey's findings are to be applied or **generalized.** Consider the two surveys shown in Example 1.1.

## EXAMPLE 1.1
### Two Surveys:
### Target Populations and Samples

*Survey 1*

*General Purpose:* To examine the attitudes of parents regarding the introduction of new dietary and nutritional programs into elementary schools

*Target Population:* All parents of children in a school district's elementary schools

*Sample:* 500 of the district's 10,000 parents (100 chosen at random from each of the district's five elementary schools)

*Survey 2*

*General Purpose:* To compare the reading habits of different users of the local library

*Target Population:* All persons who check out books from the library

*Sample:* Over the course of an allotted 6-month period, first 200 of all who check out books who complete the survey

In the first survey, 500 parents will be sampled, and their responses will be used to represent the views of the target: all parents whose children are in the district's elementary schools. In the second survey, 200 persons will represent the target population of all library users who check out books.

Why should you sample? Why not include all parents and all people who check out books? Sampling is efficient and precise. Samples can be studied more quickly than target populations, and they are also less expensive to assemble. Sampling is efficient in that resources that might go into collecting data on an unnecessarily large number of individuals or groups can be spent on other activities like monitoring the quality of data collection.

Sampling helps focus the survey on precisely the characteristics of interest. For example, if you want to compare older and younger parents of differing ethnicities, sampling strategies are available (in this case, stratified sampling) to give you just what is needed. A sample of the population with precisely defined characteristics is more suitable for many surveys than the entire population.

When selecting a sample, be sure that it is a faithful representation of the target population. No sample is perfect, however, as it usually has some degree of bias or error. The following checklist can be used in helping to ensure a sample whose characteristics and degree of representation can be described accurately.

## Checklist for Obtaining a
## Sample That Represents the Target

✓ **Survey objectives are stated precisely.**

The objectives are the reasons for doing the survey. Surveys are done to describe, compare, and predict knowledge, attitudes, and behavior. A company may survey its employees to describe and compare educational backgrounds and preferences for work schedules. A school may interview students and use the data to help predict the courses that are likely to have the most influence on future plans.

Survey data are also used to evaluate whether programs and policies have been effective. For example, management may be interested in investigating if employee morale improved 3 years after the firm's reorganization, and a school may want to know how students in a new ethics education program compare with those without such a program in terms of their goals and aspirations. If the employees are given a self-administered questionnaire and the students are interviewed, then the surveys are being used for research purposes. The term "research" is used in a very general way to include systematic inquiries or investigations.

Consider again the surveys of parents' attitudes toward nutrition programs and of the reading habits of library users, as shown in Example 1.2.

## EXAMPLE 1.2
## General Purposes, Specific Objectives, and Research Questions

### Survey 1

*General Purpose:* To examine the attitudes of parents regarding the introduction of new dietary and nutritional programs into elementary schools

*Specific Objective:* To describe and compare the attitudes of parents of differing ages, ethnicities, and knowledge of nutrition toward introducing three new dietary and nutrition plans under consideration by the school

*Specific Research Questions:*

1. What are the attitudes of parents of differing ages toward introducing three new dietary and nutrition plans?

2. What are the attitudes of parents of differing ethnicities toward introducing three new dietary and nutrition plans?

3. Do parents who know more about nutrition differ in their attitudes from other parents?

### Survey 2

*General Purpose:* To compare the reading habits of different users of the local library

*Specific Objective:* To compare reading habits among local library users of differing ages, gender, and educational attainment

*Specific Research Questions:*

1. Do differences exist in reading habits among older and younger users?

> 2. Do differences exist in reading habits among males and females?
>
> 3. Do differences exist in reading habits among people of differing educational levels?

The specific research questions are the guide to the specific questions or **items** you will include in the survey. In Survey 1, questions must be included that ask parents their age and ethnicity and test their knowledge of nutrition. In Survey 2, the respondents must be asked their age, gender, education, and reading habits.

---

### EXERCISE

Add at least one possible research question to Surveys 1 and 2 above.

### ■ POSSIBLE ANSWERS ■

For Survey 1: Do parents of older and younger children differ in their attitudes?

For Survey 2: Which are the most important factors in predicting reading habits: age, gender, and/or educational attainment?

---

✓ **Eligibility criteria are clear and definite.**

The criteria for inclusion into a survey refer to the characteristics of respondents who are eligible for participation in the survey; the exclusion criteria consist of characteristics that rule out certain people. You apply the inclusion and exclusion criteria to the target population. Once you remove from the target population all those who fail to meet the inclusion criteria and all those who succeed in meeting the exclusion criteria, you are left with a study population consisting of people who are eligible to participate. Consider the illustrations in Example 1.3.

## EXAMPLE 1.3
## Inclusion and Exclusion Criteria:
## Who Is Eligible?

*Research Question:* How effective is QUITNOW in helping smokers stop smoking?

*Target Population:* Smokers

*Inclusion Criteria:*
- Between the ages of 18 and 64 years
- Smoke one or more cigarettes daily
- Have an alveolar breath carbon monoxide determination of more than eight parts per million

*Exclusion Criterion:* If any of the contraindications for the use of nicotine gum are applicable

*Comment:* The survey's results will apply only to the respondents who are eligible to participate. If a smoker is under 18 years of age or 65 or over, then the survey's findings may not apply to these people. Although the target population is smokers, the inclusion and exclusion criteria have defined their own world, or study population, as "people who smoke."

*Research Question:* Are parents satisfied with the new reading curriculum?

*Target Population:* Parents with children in elementary school

*Inclusion Criteria:*
- Have a child who has spent at least 6 months in one of the district's elementary schools as of April 15
- English or Spanish speaking

*Exclusion Criterion:* Inability or unwillingness to participate in a telephone or face-to-face interview in the four weeks beginning May 1

*Comment:* The target population is parents with children in elementary school. Parents who do not speak English or Spanish or who are unable to participate in an interview are not eligible to be part of the study population.

Both of the above surveys set boundaries for the respondents who are eligible. In so doing, they are limiting the generalizability of the findings. Why deliberately limit applicability?

A major reason for setting eligibility criteria is that to do otherwise is simply not practical. Including everyone under 18 and 65 and over in the survey of smokers requires additional resources for administering, analyzing, and interpreting data from large numbers of people. Also, very young and very old smokers' needs may be different from the majority of adult smokers. For the second survey, including parents who speak languages other than English and Spanish requires translation of the survey, an often difficult and costly task. Setting inclusion and exclusion criteria is an efficient way of focusing the survey on just those people from whom you are equipped to get the most accurate information.

<hr>

## EXERCISE

*Directions:* Set inclusion and exclusion criteria for the survey of library users described in Example 1.1, Survey 2.

### ■ POSSIBLE ANSWERS ■

*Inclusion Criteria:*
- Must use the library within a 6-month period beginning with today's date
- Must check out a book for 24 hours or more
- Must hold a permanent library card

*Exclusion Criterion:* Not a member of the local community
(e.g., relying on interlibrary loans)

<hr>

## ✓ Rigorous sampling methods are chosen.

Sampling methods are usually divided into two types. The first is called probability sampling. Probability sampling provides a statistical basis for saying that a sample is representative of the study or target population.

In probability sampling, every member of the target population has a known, nonzero probability of being included in the sample. Probability sampling implies the use of random selection. Random sampling eliminates subjectivity in choosing a sample. It is a "fair" way of getting a sample.

The second type of sampling is nonprobability sampling. Nonprobability samples are chosen based on judgment regarding the characteristics of the target population and the needs of the survey. With nonprobability sampling, some members of the eligible target population have a chance of being chosen, whereas others do not. By chance, the survey's findings may not be applicable to the target group at all.

## PROBABILITY SAMPLING

### Simple Random Sampling

The first step in sampling is to obtain a **list** of eligible units composing a population from which to sample. If the sample is to be representative of the population from which it is selected, the list or **sampling frame** must include all or nearly all members of the population. In simple random sampling, every subject or unit has an equal chance of being selected from the frame or list. Members of the target population are selected one at a time and independently. Once they have been selected, they are not eligible for a second chance and are not returned to the pool. Because of this equality of opportunity, random samples are considered relatively unbiased. One typical way of selecting a simple random sample is to use a table of random numbers or a computer-generated list of random numbers and apply them to lists of prospective participants.

Suppose a table of random numbers is used to select 10 employees at random from a list containing the names of 20 employees. The 20 names are the target population, and the list of names is the sampling frame. The surveyor assigns each name on the list a number from 01 to 20 (e.g., Adams = 01; Baker = 02; Zinsser = 20). Then, using a table of random numbers (found in practically all statistics books), the surveyor chooses the first 10 digits between 01 and 20. A second way is for the surveyor to use a computer to generate 10 numbers between 01 and 20. Suppose the numbers chosen at random are 01, 03, 05, 06, 12, 14, 15, 17, 19, and 20. Employees' names with the corresponding numbers are included in the sample. For example, Adams and Zinsser with numbers 01 and 20 are included; Baker with number 02 is not.

The advantage of simple random sampling is that you can get an unbiased sample without much technical difficulty. Unfortunately, random sampling may not pick up all the elements in a population that are of interest. Suppose you are conducting a survey of patient satisfaction. Consider also that you have evidence from a previous study that older and younger patients usually differ substantially in their satisfaction. If you choose a simple random sample for your new survey, you might not pick up a large enough proportion of younger patients to detect any differences that matter in your particular survey. To be sure that you get adequate proportions of people with certain characteristics, you need stratified random sampling.

## Stratified Random Sampling

A stratified random sample is one in which the population is divided into subgroups or "strata," and a random sample is then selected from each subgroup. For example, suppose you want to find out about the effectiveness of a program to teach men about options for treatment for prostate cancer. You plan to survey a sample of 1,800 of the 3,000 men who have participated in the program. You also intend to divide the men into groups according to their general health status (as indicated by scores on a 32-item test), age, and income (high = +, medium = 0, and low = −). Health status, age, and income are the strata.

The sampling blueprint for the survey of men to find out about their program is given in Example 1.4.

**EXAMPLE 1.4**
## Sampling Blueprint for a
## Program to Educate Men in
## Options for Prostate Cancer Treatment

| Scores and Income | Age (Years) | | | | | |
|---|---|---|---|---|---|---|
| | **< 55** | **56 - 65** | **66 - 70** | **71 - 75** | **> 75** | **Total** |
| **25 - 32 points** | | | | | | |
| High income | 30 | 30 | 30 | 30 | 30 | 150 |
| Average | 30 | 30 | 30 | 30 | 30 | 150 |
| Low | 30 | 30 | 30 | 30 | 30 | 150 |
| **17 - 24 points** | | | | | | |
| High income | 30 | 30 | 30 | 30 | 30 | 150 |
| Average | 30 | 30 | 30 | 30 | 30 | 150 |
| Low | 30 | 30 | 30 | 30 | 30 | 150 |
| **9 - 16 points** | | | | | | |
| High income | 30 | 30 | 30 | 30 | 30 | 150 |
| Average | 30 | 30 | 30 | 30 | 30 | 150 |
| Low | 30 | 30 | 30 | 30 | 30 | 150 |

| | Age (Years) | | | | | |
|---|---|---|---|---|---|---|
| **Scores and Income** | **< 55** | **56 - 65** | **66 - 70** | **71 - 75** | **> 75** | **Total** |
| 1 - 8 points | | | | | | |
| High income | 30 | 30 | 30 | 30 | 30 | 150 |
| Average | 30 | 30 | 30 | 30 | 30 | 150 |
| Low | 30 | 30 | 30 | 30 | 30 | 150 |
| Total | 360 | 360 | 360 | 360 | 360 | 1,800 |

How do you decide on subgroups? The strata or subgroups are chosen because evidence is available that they are related to the outcome, in this case, the options chosen by men with prostate cancer. That is, proof exists that general health status, age, and income influence a man's choice. The justification for the selection of the strata can come from the literature and expert opinion.

Stratified random sampling is more complicated than simple random sampling. The strata must be identified and justified, and using many subgroups can lead to large, unwieldy, and expensive surveys.

## Systematic Sampling

Suppose you have a list of the names of 3,000 customers from which a sample of 500 is to be selected for a marketing survey. Dividing 3,000 by 500 yields 6. That means that 1 of every 6 persons will be in the sample. To systematically sample from the list, a random start is needed. To obtain this, a die can be tossed. Suppose the toss comes up with the number 5. This means that the 5th name on the list is selected first, then the 11th, 17th, 23rd, and so on until 500 names are selected.

Systematic sampling should not be used if repetition is a natural component of the sampling frame. For example, if the frame is a list of names, systematic sampling can result in the loss of names that appear infrequently (e.g., names beginning with X). If the data are arranged by months, and the interval is 12, the same months will be selected for each year. Infrequently appearing names and ordered data (January is always Month 1 and December Month 12) prevents each sampling unit (names or months) from having an equal chance of selection. If systematic sampling is used without the guarantee that all units have an equal chance of selection, the resultant sample will not be a probability sample. When the sampling frame has no inherently recurring order, or you can reorder the list or adjust the sampling intervals, systematic sampling resembles simple random sampling.

## Cluster Sampling

A cluster is a naturally occurring unit like a school (which has many classrooms, students, and teachers). Other clusters are universities, hospitals, cities, states, and so on. The clusters are randomly selected, and all members of the selected cluster are included in the sample. For example, suppose that California's counties are trying out a new program to improve emergency care for critically ill and injured children. If you want to use cluster sampling, you can consider each county as a cluster and select and assign counties at random to the new children's emergency care program or to the traditonal one.

The programs in the selected counties would then be the focus of the survey.

Cluster sampling is used in large surveys. It differs from stratified sampling in that you start with a naturally occurring constituency. You then select from among the clusters and either survey all members of the selection or randomly select from among them. With stratified sampling, you create the groups. The difference between the two is illustrated in the two hypothetical cases given in Example 1.5.

---

### EXAMPLE 1.5
### Stratified and
### Cluster Sampling Contrasted

*Case 1: Stratified Sampling*

The employees of Microsell were grouped according to their departments, such as sales, marketing, research, and advertising. Ten employees were selected at random from each department.

*Case 2: Cluster Sampling*

Five of the Foremost Hotel chain's 10 hotels were chosen at random. All employees in the five hotels were surveyed.

---

Multistage sampling is an extension of cluster sampling in which clusters are selected and a sample drawn from the cluster members by simple random sampling. Clustering and sampling can be done at any stage. Example 1.6 illustrates the use of cluster sampling in a survey of Italian parents' attitudes toward AIDS.

## EXAMPLE 1.6
## Cluster Sampling and
## Attitudes of Italian Parents Toward AIDS

Social scientists from 14 of Italy's 21 regions surveyed parents of 725 students from 30 schools chosen by a cluster sample technique of the 292 classical, scientific, and technical high schools in Rome. The staff visited the schools and selected students by using a list of random numbers based on the school's size. The selected students were given a letter addressed to their parents explaining the goals of the study and stating when they would be contacted.

Cluster sampling and multistage sampling are efficient ways of collecting survey information when it is either impossible or impractical to compile an exhaustive list of the units comprising the target population. For example, it is unlikely that you can readily obtain a list of all patients in city hospitals, members of sporting clubs, and travelers to Europe. You can more easily get lists of hospitals, official sporting clubs, and travel agents.

A general guideline to follow in multistage sampling is to maximize the number of clusters. As you increase the number of clusters, you can decrease the size of the sample within each. For example, suppose you plan to survey patient satisfaction with county hospitals and need a sample of 500 patients. If you include two hospitals, you will need to obtain 250 patients in each, an often logistically difficult task to accomplish when compared to obtaining 50 patients in each of 10 hospitals. In practice, you will have to decide which is more difficult to obtain: cooperation by hospitals or by patients?

## NONPROBABILITY SAMPLING

Nonprobability samples are created because the units appear representative or because they can be conveniently assembled. Nonprobability sampling is probably appropriate in at least three situations, as illustrated in Example 1.7.

---

### EXAMPLE 1.7
### Three Sample Reasons for
### Using Nonprobability Samples

1. *Surveys of Hard-to-Identify Groups.* A survey of the goals and aspirations of members of teenage gangs is conducted. Known gang members are asked to suggest at least three others to be interviewed.

   *Comment:* Implementing a probability sampling method in this population is not practical because of potential difficulties in obtaining cooperation and completing interviews with all eligible respondents.

2. *Surveys of Specific Groups.* A survey of patients in the state's 10 hospices asks all who are capable and willing to respond about pain and pain management.

   *Comment:* Because of ethical reasons, the surveyor may be reluctant to approach all eligible patients.

3. *Surveys in Pilot Situations.* A questionnaire is mailed to all 35 nurses who participated in a workshop to learn about the use of a computer in treating nursing home patients with fever. The results of the survey will be used in deciding whether to sponsor a formal trial and evaluation of the workshop with other nurses.

   *Comment:* The purpose of the survey is to decide whether to formally try out and evaluate the workshop. Because the data are to be used as a planning activity and not to disseminate or advocate the workshop, a nonprobability sampling method is appropriate.

---

The following are six commonly used nonprobability sampling methods.

## Convenience Sampling

A convenience sample consists of a group of individuals that is ready and available, as illustrated in Example 1.8.

### EXAMPLE 1.8
### A Convenience Sample

Where do low-income people generally obtain mental health services, and how do they pay for them? To answer this question, a survey was conducted over a 2-week period, with interviewers posted in front of five supermarkets and five churches in an urban, low-income neighborhood. During the 2 weeks, 308 people completed the 10-minute survey.

The convenience sample in this survey of use of mental health services consists of all who are willing to be interviewed. People who voluntarily answer the survey's questions may be different in important ways from those who do not, however. For example, they may be more verbal, affecting their interest in and use of mental health services. Because of the potential for bias, the findings from this survey can be applied (and with great caution) only to low-income persons whose age, education, income, and so forth are similar to those in the convenience sample.

## Snowball Sampling

This type of sampling relies on previously identified members of a group to identify other members of the population. As newly identified members name others, the sample snowballs. This technique is used when a population listing is unavailable and cannot be compiled. For example, teenaged gang members and illegal aliens might be asked to participate in snowball sampling because no membership list is available. Snowball sampling is not just used with outlaws or unpopular people, as is illustrated in Example 1.9.

### EXAMPLE 1.9
### Snowball Sampling

A mail survey's aim is to identify the competencies that should be the focus of programs to train generalist physicians for the next 20 years. A list of 50 physicians and medical educators is obtained. Each of the 50 is asked to nominate 5 others who are likely to complete the questionnaire.

## Quota Sampling

Quota sampling divides the population being studied into subgroups such as male and female and younger and older. Then, you estimate the proportion of people in each subgroup (e.g., younger and older males and younger and older females). The sample is drawn to reflect each proportion, as illustrated in Example 1.10.

## EXAMPLE 1.10
## Quota Sampling

An interview was conducted with a sample of boys and girls between the ages of 10 and 15. Based on estimates taken from the school records, the researchers calculated the proportion of children in each subgroup and made this table:

| Gender | Age (Years) | | | | | |
|---|---|---|---|---|---|---|
| | 10 | 11 | 12 | 13 | 14 | 15 |
| % Boys | 22 | 16 | 16 | 23 | 10 | 13 |
| % Girls | 12 | 25 | 12 | 24 | 10 | 7 |

Using this table, 22% of the boys and 12% of the girls in the sample should be 10 years old, 16% of the boys and 25% of the girls should be 11 years old, and so on.

For quota sampling to be effective, the proportions must be accurate. Sometimes, this accuracy is elusive. School surveys are sometimes held back by mobile and changing student populations; also, age distributions (such as those in the above table) vary considerably from school to school.

### Focus Groups

Focus groups are often used in marketing research to find out what a particular component of the public needs and will consume. They usually consist of 10 to 20 people who are brought together to represent a particular population like teens, potential customers, and members of a particular profession.

Focus groups or variations on them have been used in health and social research when the consumer, client, or patient is the focus of a survey, as illustrated in Example 1.11.

## EXAMPLE 1.11
### Focus Groups in Surveys

A preliminary version is finally available of a survey of the quality of life of men with prostate cancer. Twelve patients are asked to review the survey questionnaire. The men are asked questions like this: Are all pertinent topics covered? Can you follow the directions easily? How long does the questionnaire take to complete? The results of the focus group's discussion will be used to modify the questionnaire for administration to a large sample of men with prostate cancer.

Focus groups can result in relatively in-depth portraits of the needs and expectations of a specific population. If the group that participates is unique in unanticipated ways (e.g., more educated), its members' responses may not be applicable to the larger population.

A description of commonly used probability and nonprobability sampling methods and their benefits is presented in the following table. Some of the issues that should be resolved when using each method are also discussed.

## Commonly Used Probability
## and Nonprobability Sampling Methods

| Description | Benefits | Issues |
|---|---|---|
| **Probability Sampling**<br>*Simple random sampling*<br><br>Every unit has an equal chance of selection | Relatively simple to do | Members of a subgroup of interest may not be included in appropriate proportions |
| *Stratified random sampling*<br><br>The study population is grouped according to meaningful charac-teristics or strata | Can conduct analyses of subgroups (e.g., men and women; older and younger; East and West)<br><br>Sampling variations are lower than that for random sampling; the sample is more likely to reflect the population | Must calculate sample sizes for each subgroup<br><br>Can be time consuming and costly to implement if many subgroups are necessary |
| *Systematic sampling*<br><br>Every Xth unit on a list of eligible units is selected.<br><br>Xth can mean 5th, 6th, 23rd, and so on, deter-mined by dividing the size of the population by the desired sample size | Convenient; use existing list (e.g., of names) as a sampling frame<br><br>Similar to random sam-pling if starting point (first name chosen) is randomly divided | Must watch for recur-ring patterns within the sampling frame (e.g., names beginning with a certain letter; data arranged by month) |
| *Cluster/multistage*<br><br>Natural groups or clus-ters are sampled, with members of each se-lected group subsampled afterward | Convenient; use existing units (e.g., schools, hospitals) | |

| Description | Benefits | Issues |
|---|---|---|
| **Nonprobability Sampling** *Convenience sampling* Use of a group of individuals or units that is readily available | A practical method because you rely on readily available units (e.g., students in a school, patients in a waiting room) | Because sample is opportunistic and voluntary, participants may be unlike most of the constituents in the target population |
| *Snowball sampling* Previously identified members identify other members of the population | Useful when a list of names for sampling is difficult or impractical to obtain | Recommendations may produce a biased sample Little or no control over who is named |
| *Quota sampling* The population is divided into subgroups (e.g., men and women who are living alone, living with a partner or significant other, not living alone but not living with a partner, etc.) A sample is selected based on the proportions of subgroups needed to represent the proportions in the population | Practical if reliable data exist to describe proportions (e.g., percentage of men over a certain age living alone vs. those living with a partner) | Records must be up-to-date to get accurate proportions |
| *Focus groups* Groups of 12 to 20 people serve as representatives of the population | Useful in guiding survey development | Must be certain the relatively small group is a valid reflection of the larger group that will be surveyed |

# Statistics and Samples

## Sampling Errors

A good sample is an accurately and efficiently assembled model of the population. No matter how proficient you are, however, sampling bias or error is inevitable.

One major source of error in a sample arises from nonsampling sources. Although this may appear contradictory, the fact is that nonsampling error affects the accuracy of a survey's findings because it mars the sample's representativeness. Nonsampling error occurs because of imprecisions in the definition of the target and study population and errors in survey design and measurement.

Suppose you plan to conduct a survey of the mental health needs of homeless children. One problem you might encounter is that during the time you need for your survey, the needs may change because of historical circumstances. New health policies occurring at the same time as your survey, for example, could produce programs and services that take care of currently homeless children's most pressing needs. One way of avoiding this type of bias, that is, one that comes about because of a change in definition of needs, is to organize the survey so that its duration is not likely to encompass any major historical changes, such as alterations in policies to improve the availability of mental health services. This requires careful timing and an understanding of the political and social context in which all surveys—even small ones—take place.

A second nonsampling problem relates to definitions and inclusion and exclusion criteria. A particular survey's definitions of mental health needs and homeless will necessarily include some children and exclude others. Definitions of key survey concepts should be based on the best available theory and practice; experts may also be asked to comment on them and on the extent to which they are likely to encompass the target population.

Another source of nonsampling bias is nonresponse. Not everyone who is eligible participates; not everyone who participates answers all survey questions. A number of methods can be used to improve the response rate, such as paying respondents for their participation, sending reminder notices that a survey response is due, and protecting respondents with confidentiality and anonymity.

Biases may also be introduced by the measurement or survey process itself. Poorly worded questions and response choices, inadequately trained interviewers, and unreadable survey questionnaires contribute to the possibility of error.

Sampling errors arise from the selection process. A list of names with duplicate entries will favor some people over others, for example. Most typically, selection bias results when nonprobability sampling methods are used and not everyone has a nonzero probability of being chosen. Selection bias is insidious because it can effectively damage the credibility of your survey.

The best way to avoid selection bias is to use probability sampling methods. If you cannot, you must demonstrate that the target and sample do not differ statistically on selected but important variables, such as age, health status, and education. You can get data on these variables from vital statistics (like the census or other federal, state, and local registries) and from published reports. For example, suppose you conduct a survey of low-income women who participate in a statewide project to improve their use of prenatal care services. Without comparison data, you have no way of knowing the extent of bias in your sample, although you can be fairly sure it is there. If use of services increases, you cannot be certain that the program was the cause. The women who participated may have been more motivated to seek care to begin with than were nonparticipants. Useful comparison information may be available in the published literature on prenatal care. With it, you can find out about the patterns of use maintained by women of similar backgrounds.

---

**WARNING**

Be wary of data from other surveys and samples. Although the respondents may be alike in some respects, they may be different in others, which can be the ones that count.

All samples contain errors. Although samples are chosen to exemplify a target population, chance dictates that the two are unlikely to be identical. When you use probability sampling methods, you can calculate how much a sample varies by chance from the population.

If you draw an infinite number of samples from a population, the statistics you produce to describe the sample, like the mean (which is the numerical average), standard deviation, or proportion, will form a normal distribution around the population value. (Additional information about the mean, standard deviation, proportion, and normal distribution can be found in **How to Analyze Survey Data,** Vol. 8 in this series.) For example, suppose that the mean score in a survey of attitudes toward a bond issue is 50. An examination of an infinite number of means taken from an infinite number of samples would find the means clustering around 50. The means that are computed from each sample form a distribution of values. This distribution is called the **sampling distribution.** When the sample size reaches 30 or more participants, the distribution of the sampling means has the shape of the normal distribution. This is true no matter what the shape of the frequency distribution is of the study population, as long as a large number of samples is selected.

The sample means tend to gather closer around the true population mean with larger samples and less variation in what is being measured. The variation of the sample means around the true value is called **sampling error.** The statistic used to describe the sampling error is called the **standard error of the mean.** The difference between the standard deviation and the standard error of the mean is that the standard deviation tells how much variability can be expected among individuals. The standard error of the mean is the standard deviation of the means in a sampling distribution. It tells how much variability can be expected among means in future samples.

When the value of a standard error has been estimated, 68% of the means of samples of a given size and design will fall within the range of 1 standard error of the true population mean; 95% of the samples will fall within 2 standard errors. This is shown in Figure 2.1. When you provide survey results, you report them in terms of how confident you are that the samples fall within the range of 2 standard errors.

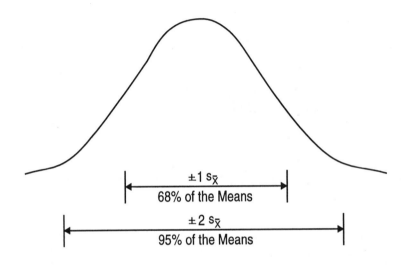

**Figure 2-1**   Sampling Distribution of the Mean

### ESTIMATING THE STANDARD ERROR
### FOR SIMPLE RANDOM SAMPLES

Although having a basic understanding of statistical notation is helpful in reading this section, "nontechnically" oriented readers should plow through to the extent possible because of the importance of the logic and principles of sampling that are discussed. Sampling is a complicated activity, and consultation with an expert is advised. However, consultation with the experts is always more satisfying and efficient if the consultee understands the vocabulary and principles.

The formula for estimating the standard error of a mean is calculated from the variance and the size of the sample from which it was estimated:

$$SE = \sqrt{Var/n} \, ,$$

where

$$\sqrt{\phantom{x}} \quad = \quad \text{square root}$$

SE   =   standard error of the mean

Var  =   variance (sum of the squared deviations
         from the sample mean over $n$)

$n$   =   number of individuals comprising the sample

Surveys typically report proportions or percentages of respondents answering yes or no. For example, 20% of the respondents say "yes" when asked if they understand the difference between the standard deviation and the standard error, and 80% say "no." One way of thinking about the proportion is as the mean of a two-value distribution.

A mean is the average. The formula for calculating the sample mean is

$$\overline{X} = \Sigma X/n,$$

where

$\overline{X}$   =   mean (numerical average)

$\Sigma$   =   sum of (Greek letter sigma)

$X$   =   number of observations
        (e.g., number of people answering yes)

$n$   =   sample size (e.g., number of people who
        answered the question)

Suppose you have two values: 1 = yes and 0 = no. You have 100 people in the sample, and 20 say yes and 80 say no. The mean of the two values—20 and 80—can be calculated this way:

$$\Sigma X = 20 \times 1 + 80 \times 0 = 20;$$
$$\Sigma X/n = 20/100 = .20.$$

A proportion or percentage (e.g., 20% say they do not understand the difference between standard deviations and errors) is a statement about the mean of a 1/0 distribution, and the mean is .20.

The formula for calculating the standard error of a proportion includes the following:

$$p(1 - p),$$

where

$$p \quad = \quad \text{proportion with the characteristic}$$
$$\text{(e.g., 20% yes)}$$
$$(1 - p) \quad = \quad \text{proportion without the characteristic}$$
$$\text{(e.g., 80% no)}$$

To calculate the standard error of a proportion, start with the formula for the standard error of the mean ( $\sqrt{Var/n}$ ). The variation for the proportion is $p(1 - p)$, and so the formula for the standard error of a proportion becomes

$$\sqrt{p(1 - p)/n} \ .$$

With 20% of a 100-person sample understanding the difference between standard deviations and standard errors, the standard error would be

$$\sqrt{p(1 - p)/n} = \sqrt{(.20 \times .80)/100} = \sqrt{.16/100} = .04.$$

If you add .04 to the yes vote and also subtract .04 from it, you have an interval from .24 to .16. You can say that the probability is .68 (1 standard error from the sample mean) that the true population figure is within that interval. If you want to be 95% confident, then you must add 2 standard errors, and the interval now becomes .28 to .12. You can now say that you are 95% confident that the true population mean is between .28 and .12.

The following table gives you the estimated sampling error for a percentage of a sample that has a certain "binomial" characteristic (under 19 years of age or over; male or female) or provides a certain response (yes or no; agree or do not agree). You use the table by finding the connection between the sample size and the approximate percentage for each characteristic or response. The number appearing at the connection is the estimated sampling error at the 95% confidence level.

| Sample Size | Binomial (yes, no; on, off) Percentage Distribution | | | | |
| | 50/50 | 60/40 | 70/30 | 80/20 | 90/10 |
| --- | --- | --- | --- | --- | --- |
| 100 | 10 | 9.8 | 9.2 | 8 | 6 |
| 200 | 7.1 | 6.9 | 6.5 | 5.7 | 4.2 |
| 300 | 5.8 | 5.7 | 5.3 | 4.6 | 3.5 |
| 400 | 5 | 4.9 | 4.6 | 4 | 3 |
| 500 | 4.5 | 4.4 | 4.1 | 3.6 | 2.7 |
| 600 | 4.1 | 4 | 3.7 | 3.3 | 2.4 |
| 700 | 3.8 | 3.7 | 3.5 | 3 | 2.3 |
| 800 | 3.5 | 3.5 | 3.3 | 2.8 | 2.1 |
| 900 | 3.3 | 3.3 | 3.1 | 2.7 | 2 |
| 1,000 | 3.2 | 3.1 | 3 | 2.5 | 1.9 |
| 1,100 | 3 | 3 | 2.8 | 2.4 | 1.8 |
| 1,200 | 2.9 | 2.8 | 2.6 | 2.3 | 1.7 |
| 1,300 | 2.8 | 2.7 | 2.5 | 2.2 | 1.7 |
| 1,400 | 2.7 | 2.6 | 2.4 | 2.1 | 1.6 |
| 1,500 | 2.6 | 2.5 | 2.4 | 2.1 | 1.5 |
| 1,600 | 2.5 | 2.4 | 2.3 | 2 | 1.5 |
| 1,700 | 2.4 | 2.4 | 2.2 | 1.9 | 1.4 |
| 1,800 | 2.4 | 2.3 | 2.2 | 1.9 | 1.4 |
| 1,900 | 2.3 | 2.2 | 2.1 | 1.8 | 1.3 |
| 2,000 | 2.2 | 2.2 | 2 | 1.8 | 1.3 |

Example 2.1 gives an illustration of how to use the tables.

## EXAMPLE 2.1
## How to Establish Confidence Intervals

In a survey of 100 respondents, 70% answer yes and 30% answer no. According to the preceding table, the sampling error is ±9.2 percentage points. Adding 9.2 and subtracting 9.2 from the 70% who say yes, you get a confidence interval between 79.2% and 60.8%. You can estimate with 95% confidence that the proportion of the sample saying yes is somewhere in the interval.

### EXERCISES

1. In a survey of 200 respondents, 60% say yes. What is the confidence interval for a 95% confidence level?
2. In a survey of 150 respondents, 90% say yes. What is the confidence interval for a 95% confidence level?

### ■ ANSWERS ■

1. 53.1% to 69.8% (interval of 9.8%)
2. About 85% to 95% (interval of about 5%)

Remember that the table only applies to errors due to sampling. Other sources of error, like nonsampling errors or nonresponse, are not reflected in this table. Also, the table only works for simple random samples. For other sampling methods and confidence levels, a more advanced knowledge of statistics is required than is assumed here.

## Sample Size: How Much Is Enough?

The size of the sample refers to the numbers of units that need to be surveyed to get precise and reliable findings. The units can be people (e.g., men and women over and under 45 years of age), places (e.g., counties, hospitals, schools), and things (e.g., medical or school records).

The influence of increasing sample size on sampling variation or standard error is shown in Figure 2.2.

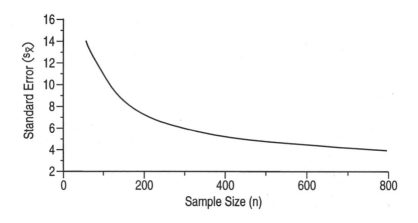

**Figure 2-2**   Sample Size and Sample Variation

The figure shows that sampling variability decreases as the sample size increases. The gain in precision is greater for each unit increase in the smaller sample size range than in the larger.

When you increase the sample's size, you increase its cost. Larger samples mean increased costs for data collection (especially for interviews), data processing, and analysis. Moreover, increasing the sample size may divert attention from other sampling activities like following up on eligible people who fail to respond. The diversion may actually increase total sampling error. It is very important to remember that many factors affect the amount of error or chance variation in the sample. Besides nonresponse, one of these is the design of a sample. If the sample design deviates from simple random sampling, relies on cluster sampling, or does not use probability sampling, then the total error will invariably decrease the quality of the survey's findings. The size of the sample, although a leading contender in the sampling error arena, is just one of several factors to consider in coming up with a "good" sample.

The most appropriate way to produce the right sample size is to use statistical calculations. These can be relatively complex, depending on the needs of the survey. Some surveys have just one sample, and others have several. Like most survey activities, sample size considerations should be placed within a broad context. The following checklist of factors to account for when considering sample size is useful.

---

## Checklist of Factors to Consider When Calculating Sample Size

✓ **Assemble and clarify all survey objectives, questions, or hypotheses.**

Before you begin to consider the size of the sample, you must decide on the objectives, questions, or hypotheses that the survey is to answer. Consider these:

- Survey 1: Quality of Life

  *Objective:* To determine if younger and older women differ in their quality of life after surgery for breast cancer

  *Question:* Do younger and older women differ in their quality of life after surgery for breast cancer?

  *Hypothesis:* Younger and older women do not differ in their quality of life after surgery for breast cancer.

- Survey 2: Fear in School

  *Objective:* To determine if students in urban schools are more fearful of violence or tests

  *Question:* Which do students in urban schools fear more: violence or tests?

  *Hypothesis:* Students in urban schools fear violence more than tests.

- Survey 3: Use of Mental Health Services

  *Objective:* To determine which of the following reasons account for ethnic/racial differences in the use of mental health services

  *Question:* Which of the following reasons account for ethnic/racial differences in the use of mental health services?

  *Hypothesis:* Lack of knowledge regarding where to go for services predicts underuse of services among African Americans.

- Survey 4: Attitude Toward Dieting and Exercising

  *Objective:* To determine if a difference exists in attitude toward dieting and exercising and knowledge of health among men and women of differing ages after participation in the company's new and traditional health-promotion/risk-reduction programs

*Question:* Does a difference exist in attitude toward dieting and exercising and knowledge of health among men and women of differing ages after participation in the company's new and traditional health-promotion/risk-reduction programs?

*Hypothesis:* After participation in the company's new and traditional health-promotion/risk-reduction programs, differences exist among men and women of differing ages in attitude toward dieting and exercising but not in knowledge of health.

The objectives, questions and hypotheses are illustrations. Little difference exists in how they are stated. Hypotheses, however, require special handling; this is discussed later.

Each objective, question, and hypothesis contains the independent and dependent variables. Independent variables, the "grouping variables," are used to predict or explain the dependent variables. Take the question "Do boys and girls differ in their attitudes toward school?" The grouping or independent variable is gender. The hidden question is whether knowledge of gender predicts attitudes. In statistical terms, the independent variables specify the conditions under which estimates of or inferences about the dependent variable are to be made.

The dependent variables are the attitudes, behaviors, and knowledge the survey is measuring. In statistical terms, they are the variables for which estimates are to be made or inferences drawn. In the question "Do boys and girls differ in their attitudes toward school?" the dependent variable is attitudes toward school.

Independent and dependent variables can be divided into categories or levels. Gender has two categories: male and female. The independent and dependent variables of the four surveys above are described in the following table.

|                | **Independent Variable**                                                                                              | **Dependent Variable**                                                                              |
| -------------- | --------------------------------------------------------------------------------------------------------------------- | --------------------------------------------------------------------------------------------------- |
| Survey 1       | Age of women: older and younger                                                                                       | Quality of life                                                                                     |
| Survey 2       | Students in urban schools                                                                                             | Fear: of violence and tests                                                                         |
| Survey 3       | Ethnic/racial groups (e.g., African American, Latino, White, Asian Pacific Islander, Chinese, Japanese)              | Use of mental health services                                                                       |
| Survey 4       | Health-promotion programs: new and traditional; gender: male and female; age: from youngest to oldest employee        | Attitude toward dieting and exercising; knowledge of the effects of diet and exercise               |

## ✓ Identify subgroups.

The subgroups refer to the groups in the sample whose survey results must be obtained in sufficient numbers for accurate conclusions. In the four surveys above, the subgroups can be identified by looking at the independent variables. Survey 1's subgroups are older and younger women, Survey 3's are ethnic and racial groups (e.g., African American, Latino), and Survey 4's are new and traditional programs and males and females and youngest to oldest employees. Survey 2 does not specify subgroups.

## ✓ Identify survey type and data collection needs.

The dependent variables signal the content of the survey. For example, Survey 1's questions will ask respondents about various aspects of their quality of life, Survey 2's will ask about fear in school, Survey 3's about use of mental health services, and Survey 4's about attitudes toward diet and exercise and knowledge of health. For illustrative purposes, assume that Survey 1 is a face-to-face interview, Survey 2 a self-administered questionnaire, Survey 3 a telephone interview, and Survey 4 a face-to-face interview.

Interviews and self-administered questionnaires have specific and general data collection needs. The specific needs will vary according to the survey's situation. For example, the survey about use of mental health services may need to be translated into more than one language, and the survey about fear in school may need to be anonymous. General data collection needs refer to those that are inherent in the survey method itself. For instance, face-to-face interviews require extensive interviewer training and are labor intensive. With mailed questionnaires, although the initial costs of paper and postage may be low, the costs of follow-up and nonresponse may be high.

## ✓ Check the survey's resources and schedule.

A survey with many subgroups and measures will be more complex and costly than those with few. Consider Example 2.2.

## EXAMPLE 2.2
### Subgroups, Measures,
### Resources, and Schedule

|  | Subgroups | Type of Survey | Comments |
|---|---|---|---|
| *Survey 1:*<br>Do younger and older women differ in their quality of life after surgery for breast cancer? | Younger and older women: 2 subgroups | Face-to-face interview | May need time to hire and train different interviewers for younger and older women<br><br>May have difficulty recruiting sufficient numbers of eligible younger or older women |
| *Survey 2:*<br>Are students in urban schools more fearful of violence or tests? | Students in urban schools: 1 group | Self-administered questionnaire | May need time to translate the questionnaire from English into other languages<br><br>Must decide whether to have confidential or anonymous questionnaires |
| *Survey 3:*<br>Which of the following reasons account for ethnic/racial differences in the use of mental health services? | Race/ethnicity: African American, White, Latino, Chinese, Japanese, Southeast Asian, Asian Pacific Islander: 7 subgroups | Telephone interview | May need time to hire and train interviewers who speak many languages |

| | Subgroups | Type of Survey | Comments |
|---|---|---|---|
| *Survey 4:*<br>Does a difference in attitude toward dieting and exercising and knowledge of health exist among men and women of differing ages after participation in the company's new and traditional heath-promotion/risk-reduction programs? | Men and women of five differing ages; new and traditional programs: 12 subgroups | Face-to-face interview | Will have to administer one survey with a knowledge and an attitude component or two separate surveys<br><br>May need time to find or develop the survey |

The number of subgroups in Example 2.2 ranges from 1 to 12. Administering a survey to one group is difficult enough; 12 groups increase the difficulty. Relatively more time and other resources are usually needed, especially if you intend to conduct statistical analyses.

To picture the complexity of many survey groups, consider Survey 4 in Example 2.2. This survey has 12 subgroups: new program, traditional program, men of five ages, and women of five ages. This is illustrated in the sampling blueprint given in Example 2.3.

## EXAMPLE 2.3
## Sampling Blueprint

|  | New Program | | Traditional Program | |
|---|---|---|---|---|
| **Years of Age** | **Men** | **Women** | **Men** | **Women** |
| 20 - 25 |  | * |  | * |
| 26 - 30 |  |  |  |  |
| 31 - 40 |  |  |  |  |
| 41 - 55 |  |  |  |  |
| Over 55 | * |  |  |  |

NOTE: Asterisks (*) are guides in reading the blueprint. They represent women between 20 and 25 in the new program, women between 20 and 25 in the traditional program, and men over 55 in the new program.

A sampling blueprint provides a pictorial representation of the sampling plan. The blueprint in Example 2.3 is a picture of the groups that are to be surveyed in order to answer the question "Does a difference in attitude toward dieting and exercising and knowledge of health exist among men and women of differing ages (defined in the blueprint as between 20 and 25, 26 and 30, 31 and 40, 41 and 55, and over 55) after participation in the company's new and traditional health-promotion/risk-reduction programs?"

Each of the subgroups is represented by an empty box or **cell**. Three subgroups are marked by an asterisk as examples. To achieve this configuration of subgroups, you can use stratified random sampling. If you were comparing attitudes after participation in the new and traditional program, a statistical rule-of-thumb suggests that you need about 30 people in each group. As soon as you increase the number of cells or subgroups, you also need to increase the sample's size to have at least 30 in each subgroup. This is shown in Example 2.4 in two hypothetical cases. In Case 1, the new and traditional programs are compared, and 60 people are needed. In Case 2, men and women are compared in each program, and 120 people are needed.

### EXAMPLE 2.4
### More Subgroups and Larger Samples

*Case 1*

| New Program | Traditional Program | Total |
|---|---|---|
| Sample = 30 | Sample = 30 | Sample = 60 |

*Case 2*

| New Program | | Traditional Program | | |
|---|---|---|---|---|
| Men | Women | Men | Women | Total |
| Sample = 30 | Sample = 30 | Sample = 30 | Sample = 30 | Sample = 120 |

A large number of groups and measures increase the costs of the survey and the time needed to complete it. If the survey's resources and schedule are incompatible with the survey's aspirations, a compromise is necessary.

# Calculating Sample Size

The ideal sample is a miniature version of the target population. To achieve this ideal means using techniques to avoid biases due to nonsampling and design errors. Nonsampling errors arise from poor definitions of the target and nonresponse. Design errors occur when sample selection deviates from probability techniques. The ideal sample is also large enough to detect effects or changes. Several different formulas may be used to estimate sample sizes; in fact, a number of books are devoted to the subject.

Suppose a survey is concerned with finding out whether a program is effective in improving the health, education, and quality of life for adolescents. Assume also that one survey objective is to compare the goals and aspirations of adolescents in the program with adolescents who are not in the program. How large should each group of adolescents be? To answer this question, five other questions must be answered.

---

# Checklist of Questions to Ask When Determining Sample Size

### ✓ What is the null hypothesis?

The null hypothesis $(H_0)$ is a statement that no difference exists between the average or mean scores of two groups. For example, one null hypothesis for the survey of adolescents is that no difference exists between goals and aspirations (as measured by average survey scores) between adolescents participating in the program and nonparticipants.

✓ **What is the desired level of significance (α level) related to the null hypothesis involving the mean in the population (μ₀)?**

NOTE: In hypothesis testing, you use the mean in the population ($\mu$, or Greek letter mu) rather than the mean in the sample ($\overline{X}$).

The level of significance, when chosen before the test is performed, is called the alpha value (denoted by Greek letter $\alpha$). The alpha gives the probability of rejecting the null hypothesis when it is actually true. Tradition keeps the alpha value small—.05, .01, or .001—to avoid rejecting a null hypothesis when it is true (and no difference exists between group means). The *p* value is the probability that an observed result (or result of a statistical test) is due to chance (rather than to participation in a program). It is calculated **AFTER** the statistical test. If the *p* value is less than alpha, then the null is rejected.

✓ **What chance should there be of detecting an actual difference? Put another way, what is the power (1 – β, or Greek letter beta) associated with the alternative hypothesis involving μ₁?**

When differences are found to exist between two groups, and, in reality, there are no differences, that is called an alpha, or Type I, error. When no differences are found between groups, although in reality there are differences, that is termed a beta, or Type II, error. These relationships are shown in the following table.

Truth

|  | Differences Exist | No Differences Exist |
|---|---|---|
| Differences exist (reject null) | Correct | Type I or alpha error |
| No differences exist (keep null) | Type II or beta error | Correct |

**Conclusions From Hypothesis Test**

### ✓ What differences between the means must be detected to be important? That is, what is a meaningful $\mu_1 - \mu_2$?

Suppose the survey uses the Goals and Aspirations Scale. This hypothetical scale has 50 points. The first step in the use of this (or another survey searching for differences) is to agree on a difference between means that is important in practical and statistical terms. To decide on importance, you can seek expert guidance and ask a question like "Will a 5-point difference matter? Will 10 points?" (This difference is sometimes referred to as the "effect," and the size of the difference is the "effect size.")

### ✓ What is a good estimate of the standard deviation σ in the population?

The standard deviation (denoted by lowercase Greek letter sigma, or σ) is a common measure of dispersion or spread of data about the mean. Two general rules apply to the standard deviation. First, at least 75% of all values (such as scores) always lie between the mean and 2 standard deviations. If 100 people complete a survey, their mean score is 25, and the standard deviation is 2, then at least 75 respondents will have scores of $25 \pm 4$. That is, their scores will fall between 21 and 29.

If the distribution of values or observations is a bell-shaped or normal distribution, then 68% of the observations will fall between the mean ±1 standard deviation, 95% of the observations between ±2 standard deviations, and 99% of the observations between ±3 standard deviations.

Estimates of the standard deviation can come from previously done surveys, but before using it, check that the population is similar to your own. If not, the standard deviation is also likely to be different. You can conduct a small pilot test using about 25 people and calculate the standard deviation. Finally, you can have experts give you estimates on the highest and lowest values or scores as the basis for calculating the standard deviation.

The formula for calculating sample size for comparing the means from two independent groups (e.g., adolescents participating in a program to improve their health and education vs. nonparticipants) is given below. This is one of many formulas that might be used in calculating sample size for surveys, as the aim of all formulas is to provide enough survey respondents to produce accurate findings. This formula assumes that the standard deviations in the two populations are equal and the sample sizes are equal in the two groups:

$$\frac{(z_\alpha - z_\beta)\sigma^2}{\mu_1 - \mu_2} ,$$

where

$$\mu_1 - \mu_2 \quad = \quad \text{magnitude of the difference to be detected between the two groups,}$$

$$z_\alpha \quad = \quad \text{upper tail in the normal distribution, and}$$

$$z_\beta \quad = \quad \text{lower tail in the normal distribution).}$$

These "tails" are defined as

$$z_\alpha = \frac{X - \mu_1}{\sigma/\sqrt{n}} \quad \text{and} \quad z_\beta = \frac{X - \mu_2}{\sigma/\sqrt{n}}.$$

Example 2.5 gives an illustration of the application of the formula.

## EXAMPLE 2.5
### Calculating Sample Size in a Survey of Adolescents in an Experimental and Control Group

**Survey Situation**

Two groups of adolescents are participating in a program to improve their health, education, and quality of life. At the conclusion of the 3-year program, participants in the experimental and control groups will be surveyed to find out about their goals and aspirations. The highest score on the survey is 100 points. The Type I error or alpha level is set at .05. The probability of detecting a true difference is set at .80. Experts in adolescent behavior say that the difference in scores between the experimental and control groups (the size of the effect) should be 10 points or more. Previous experiments using the survey have revealed a standard deviation of 15 points.

**Calculations**

For the calculation, let us assume that a standard normal distribution or z distribution is appropriate. The standard normal curve has a mean of 0 and a standard deviation of 1. The two-tailed z value related to $\alpha = .05$ is 1.96 (for more about the standard normal distribution, one- and two-tailed tests, and z values, see **How to Analyze Survey Data,** Vol. 8 in this series; actual z values are obtainable in any elementary statistics book). For $\alpha = .01$, the two-tailed z value is 2.58; for $\alpha = .10$, 1.65; and for $\alpha = .20$, 1.28.

The lower one-tailed z value related to β is −.84 (the critical value or z score separating the lower 20% of the z distribution from 80%). Applying the formula

$$(1.96 + 0.84)(15)^2 = 2\left(\frac{42}{10}\right)^2$$

2(17.64), or about 36.

At least 36 adolescents are needed in each group to have an 80% chance of detecting a difference in scores of 10 points.

## Sampling Units and the Unit of Analysis

The sampling unit is the individual, group, or other entity that is selected for the survey or assigned to groups. The unit of analysis is the entity whose survey data are examined statistically. Sometimes, sampling and analysis units are the same; at other times, they are not. In simple one-stage sampling, they are the same; in more complex multistage samples, they are not, as illustrated in Example 2.6.

### EXAMPLE 2.6
### Sampling Units and the Unit of Analysis:
### Sometimes the Same and Sometimes Not

*Case 1: Sampling Unit and Unit of Analysis Are the Same*

*Survey Objective:* To determine if the program ENHANCE has improved students' attitudes toward school

*Sampling Method:* Names of 500 eligible students are compiled from school records. From the list, 200 names are randomly selected. Of these, 100 students are randomly assigned to the experimental program and 100 are assigned to the control program.

*Survey Instrument:* A 10-item self-administered questionnaire. A positive answer to a question means a favorable response.

*Statistical Analysis:* The number of positive answers on each questionnaire is added to come up with a score. The average score in the experimental and control groups is computed. A comparison is made between each group's average score to test for statistical differences.

*Sampling Unit:* The student (individual students are selected; individual students are assigned)

*Unit of Analysis:* The student (each student's questionnaire is scored, and the scores are aggregated and averaged across students)

## Case 2: Sampling Unit and Unit of Analysis Are Different

*Survey Objective:* To determine if the program ENHANCE has improved students' attitudes toward school

*Sampling Method:* Four elementary schools are selected because they represent the district's 14 schools in terms of enrollment size and family demographies (e.g., socioeconomic indicators). The four schools are grouped into two pairs, AB and CD. A 30% sample of second-grade classrooms (16 classrooms totaling 430 students) in the first members of the two pairs of schools is selected at random from the total second-grade enrollment to receive the experimental program in the first semester. A 20% random sample of second-grade classrooms (10 classrooms totaling 251 students) in the second members of the two pairs serves as the comparison or control group (receiving no formal program). Similarly, a 30% sample of fourth-grade classrooms (13 classrooms totaling 309 students) in the second members of the two pairs of schools is selected at random from the total fourth-grade enrollment to receive the special program curriculum in the first semester, and a 20% random sample of the fourth-grade enrollment (13 classrooms totaling 326 students) in the first members of the two pairs serves as the control. Of the 1,316 students participating, 739 students are assigned to the experimental program and 577 to the control. The sampling strategy provides a greater than 80% power to detect a "small" treatment difference, holding a Type I error at 5%. The sampling strategy can be graphically illustrated as follows:

| | Experimental Group | | Control Group | |
|---|---|---|---|---|
| Schools | AB | CD | AB | CD |
| Grade | 2 | 4 | 4 | 2 |
| Semester | First | Second | Second | First |
| % Sample | 30 | 30 | 20 | 20 |
| No. Classrooms | 16 | 13 | 13 | 10 |
| No. Students | 430 | 309 | 326 | 251 |
| *Sample size* | | | | |
| Classrooms | 29 | | 23 | |
| Students | 739 | | 577 | |

*Survey Instrument:* A 10-item self-administered questionnaire. A positive answer to a question means a favorable response.

*Statistical Analysis:* The number of positive answers on each questionnaire is added to come up with a score. The average score in the experimental and control groups is computed. A comparison is made between each group's average score to test for statistical differences.

*Sampling Units:* The school and the classroom (schools are selected; classrooms are selected and assigned)

*Unit of Analysis:* The student (each student's questionnaire is scored, and the scores are aggregated across students)

The small number of schools and classrooms in the survey discussed in Case 2 precludes their use as the unit of statistical analysis: Larger samples are needed to detect any existing differences. However, the number of students provides a sample with power greater than 80% to detect a "small" treatment difference, holding a Type I error at 5%.

The sampling method described in Case 2 has several potential biases. First, the small numbers of schools and classrooms may result in initial differences that may strongly influence the outcome of the program. Second, students in each school or classroom may perform as a unit primarily because they have the same teacher or were placed in the classroom because of their similar abilities or interests.

When the unit of analysis is different from the sampling unit, you are often called on to demonstrate statistically or logically that your results are similar to those that would have been obtained had both units been the same. If the analysis finds initial group differences in baseline levels and demographic factors, for example, you may be able to use statistical methods to "adjust" program effects in view of the differences (for more information on statistics, see **How to Analyze Survey Data**, Vol. 8 in this series).

# Acceptable Response Rate

All surveys hope for a high response rate. No single rate is considered the standard, however. In some surveys, between 95% and 100% is expected; in others, 70% is adequate. Consider the five cases in Example 2.7.

## EXAMPLE 2.7
## Five Cases and Five Response Rates

1. The National State Health Interview is completed by a 95% sample of all who are eligible. Health officials conclude that the 5% who do not participate probably differ from participants in their health needs and demographic characteristics. They also decide that the 95% who respond are representative of most of the state's population.

2. According to statistical calculations, the Commission on Refugee Affairs needs a sample of 100 for its mailed survey. Based on the results of previous mailings, a refusal rate of 20% to 25% is anticipated. To allow for this possibility, 125 eligible people are sent a survey.

3. A sample of employees at Uniting Airlines participate in a interview regarding their job satisfaction. A 100% response is achieved.

4. A sample of recent travelers on Uniting Airlines is sent a mailed survey. After the first mailing, a 20% response rate is achieved.

5. Parents are mailed a questionnaire about their knowledge of injury prevention for children. Each parent who sends in a completed questionnaire receives a cash payment within 2 weeks. To receive the payment, parents must complete all 25 questions on the survey. An 85% response rate is obtained.

In the first case described in Example 2.7, 5% of eligible state residents do not complete the interview. These nonrespondents may be very different in their health needs, incomes, and education compared to the 95% who do respond. When nonrespondents and respondents differ on important factors, **nonresponse bias** is introduced. In Case 1, the relatively high response rate of 95% suggests that the respondents are probably similar to most of the state's residents in the distribution of their health problems and demographics. Very high response rates in interviews often are the result of the skills of well-trained interviewers who have the opportunity for feedback and retraining, if needed.

The survey in Case 2 uses past information to estimate the probable response rate. The survey **oversamples** in the hope that the desired number of respondents will participate. Oversampling can add costs to the survey but is often necessary.

Practically all surveys are accompanied by a loss of information because of nonresponse. It is very frustrating and costly to send out a mail survey, for example, only to find that half the addressees have moved. As a guide to how much oversampling is necessary, anticipate the proportion of people who, although otherwise apparently eligible, may not turn up in the sample. For mail surveys, this can happen if the addresses are out-of-date and the mail is undeliverable. With telephone interviews, respondents may not be at home. Sometimes, people cannot be interviewed in person because they suddenly become ill.

In Case 3, a 100% response rate is obtained. Response rates are always highest if the topic is of interest to the respondents or if completion of a survey is considered part of on-the-job or professional obligation to participate in information management.

Unsolicited surveys receive the lowest fraction of responses. A 20% response for a first mailing, as in Case 4, is not uncommon. With effort, response rates can be elevated to 70% or even 80%. These efforts include follow-up mailings and use of graphically sophisticated surveys and monetary and gift incentives like pens, books, radios, music and videotapes, and so on. In some situations, as in Case 4, the adequacy of the response rates can be calculated within a range, say, of 70% to 75%.

In Case 5, parents are paid upon completion of all questions and return of the survey, and a relatively high response rate of 85% is achieved. Incentives of cash or gifts will succeed in a high return rate only if respondents who are contacted are available and able to complete the survey.

Nonresponse to an entire survey introduces error or bias. Another type of nonresponse can also introduce bias: item nonresponse. Item nonresponse occurs when respondents or survey administrators do not complete all items on a survey form. This type of bias comes about when respondents do not know the answers to certain questions or refuse to answer them because they believe them to be sensitive, embarrassing, or irrelevant. Interviewers may skip questions or fail to record an answer. In some cases, answers are made but are later rejected because they appear to make no sense. This can happen if the respondent misreads the question or fails to record all the information called for. For example, respondents may leave out their year of birth and just record the month and date.

Statistical methods may be used to "correct" for nonresponse to the entire survey or just some items. One method involves "weighting." Suppose a survey wants to compare younger (under 25 years of age) and older (26 and older) college students' career goals. A review of school records reveals that younger students constitute 40% of the population, but only 20% return their questionnaires. Using statistical methods, the 20% response rate can be weighted to become the equivalent of 40%. The accuracy of the result depends on the younger respondents being similar in their answers to the nonrespondents and different in their answers from the older students.

Another method of correcting for nonresponse is called "imputation." With imputation, values are assigned for the missing response, using the responses to other items as supplementary information.

The following guidelines can be used to promote responses, minimize response bias, and reduce survey error.

## Guidelines for Promoting Responses and Minimizing Response Bias

- Use trained interviewers. Set up a quality assurance system for monitoring quality and retraining.
- Identify a larger number of eligible respondents than you need in case you do not get the sample size you need. Be careful to pay attention to the costs.
- Use surveys only when you are fairly certain that respondents are interested in the topic.
- Keep survey responses confidential or anonymous.
- Send reminders to complete mailed surveys and make repeat phone calls.
- Provide gift or cash incentives.
- Be realistic about the eligibility criteria. Anticipate the proportion of respondents who may not be able to participate because of survey circumstances (e.g., incorrect addresses) or by chance (e.g., they suddenly get ill).

## CALCULATING THE RESPONSE RATE

The response rate is the number who respond (numerator) divided by the number of **eligible** respondents (denominator):

Response rate = Respondents/Eligible to respond.

Example 2.8 shows how to calculate the rate.

---

### EXAMPLE 2.8
### Calculating the Response Rate

A survey is mailed to 500 women as part of a study to examine the use of screening mammograms in a large health plan. The following eligibility criteria are set:

*Inclusion Criteria*
- Over 40 years of age

   Current practice restricts routine screening mammograms to women over 40.

- Visited physician in the past year

   If women visited their doctor in the past year, the survey will have access to a relatively recent mailing address.

- Can read and answer all questions by herself

*Exclusion Criteria*
- Non-English- or non-Spanish-speaking

   Nearly all women in the health plan speak English or Spanish, and the researchers do not have the resources to translate the survey into other languages.

- Diagnosed with dementing illness

  This is a mailed survey. The survey team is unwilling to use a "proxy," that is, someone to answer for the respondent. A proxy may be necessary for many people with dementing illnesses (unless mild). Application of this criterion reduces the complexity of the survey.

- Hospitalized for major physical or mental disorder at the time of the survey

  This criterion is set to avoid undeliverable mail.

The first mailing produces responses from 178 women for a response rate of 35.6% (178/500). After the second mailing, 461 women respond. The survey's response rate is 92.2% (461/500).

# Exercises

1. Name the sampling method used in each of these four scenarios.

   a. Two of four software companies are chosen to participate in a new work-at-home program. The five department heads are interviewed in each of the two companies. Six employees are selected at random and complete a self-administered questionnaire by electronic mail.

   b. The rangers at five national parks are each asked to recommend two other rangers.

   c. To be eligible, students must attend a local high school and speak English. Students with poor attendance records will be excluded. All remaining students will be surveyed.

   d. The names of all teens who have been incarcerated within the last 6 months will be written individually on a piece of paper. The names will be placed in a glass jar. A blindfolded referee will selected 10 names to serve on a focus group.

2. Draw a sampling blueprint for a survey whose objective is to answer this question:

> How do employees at five companies compare this year and last year in their preferences for work schedules?

3. Review these three sampling plans, and comment on the sources of error or bias.

a. A self-administered survey to evaluate the quality of medical care is completed by the first 100 patients who seek preventive care. The objective is to find out whether the patients are satisfied with the advice and education given to them. The results are analyzed to identify if any observed differences can be explained by a person's gender, education, or health status.

b. A questionnaire is mailed to all members of Immunity International. About 60% of the questionnaires are returned. Immunity is pleased with the return rate because most unsolicited mailed surveys rarely receive more than 50% returns on the first try.

c. Two groups of children are interviewed to find out about their television viewing habits. Both groups have been involved in a program to encourage selective viewing. One program requires more involvement than the other, and it lasts longer also. Is each program equally effective? The plan is to interview at least 100 children in each group for a total of 200 children. These numbers were chosen because a similar program surveyed 200 children and got a very high degree of cooperation.

# ANSWERS

## EXERCISE 1

1a. Multistage or cluster sampling

1b. Snowball sampling

1c. No sampling. All eligible students will be surveyed. This is the population.

1d. Random sampling

## EXERCISE 2

Sampling blueprint:

| Companies | This Year | Last Year |
|:---:|:---:|:---:|
| 1 | | |
| 2 | | |
| 3 | | |
| 4 | | |
| 5 | | |

## EXERCISE 3

3a. This survey of patients' opinions about their medical care uses a convenience sample. Convenience samples sometimes result in groups of people who are markedly different from the target population.

3b. Sampling error is a combination of nonsampling and sampling problems. In this case, the error is a nonsampling error caused by a relatively low return rate (although 60% may be high for unsolicited mailed surveys without follow-ups). Two fifths (40%) of those surveyed did not respond.

3c. A sample of 100 children in each of two groups is decided upon, based on previous sample sizes. To ensure the appropriateness of the sample size for this survey, questions like the following should be answered: How much of a difference between groups is required? What is the desired level of significance related to the null hypothesis? What chance should there be of detecting a true difference (power)? What is the standard deviation in the population? It is possible that the previous survey might serve as a guide to the selection of a sample size for the present survey. Do not automatically assume that the two are identical with respect to their objectives or expectations.

# Suggested Readings

Babbie, E. (1990). *Survey research methods*. Belmont, CA: Wadsworth.

*A basic survey research primer with example of sampling-in-practice.*

Baker, T. L. (1988). *Doing social research*. New York: McGraw-Hill.

*A "how to," with examples.*

Burnam, M. A., & Koegel, P. (1988). Methodology for obtaining a representative sample of homeless persons: The Los Angeles Skid Row study. *Evaluation Review, 12,* 117-152.

*An excellent description of how to obtain a representative sample of an elusive population.*

Campbell, D. T., & Stanley, J. C. (1963). *Experimental and quasi-experimental design for research*. Chicago: Rand McNally.

*This is a classic book on the designs that are used to structure surveys and the research studies that include them. Because design and sampling interact, this is a valuable sourcebook.*

Cook, D. C., & Campbell, D. T. (1979). *Quasi-experimentation: Design and analysis issues for field settings.* Boston: Houghton Mifflin.

*This book discusses the issues that arise in fieldwork and quasi-experimentation. It helps bring together issues that link design, sampling, and analysis.*

Dillman, D. A. (1978). *Mail and telephone surveys: The total design method.* New York: John Wiley.

*The special issues associated with mail and telephone surveys are reviewed in this book.*

Frey, J. H. (1989). *Survey research by telephone.* Newbury Park, CA: Sage.

*This book contains a good review of the sampling questions that telephone surveys raise.*

Henry, G. T. (1990). *Practical sampling.* Newbury Park, CA: Sage.

*An excellent source of information about sampling methods and sampling errors. Although statistical knowledge helps, this book is worth reading even if the knowledge is basic.*

Kalton, G. (1983). *Introduction to survey sampling.* Beverly Hills, CA: Sage.

*This is an excellent discussion of survey sampling. It requires understanding of statistics.*

Kish, L. (1965). *Survey sampling.* New York: John Wiley.

*This book is a classic and often consulted in resolving issues that arise when implementing sampling designs.*

Kraemer, H. C., & Thiemann, S. (1987). *How many subjects? Statistical power analysis in research.* Newbury Park, CA: Sage.

*Although this book requires an understanding of statistics, the complexity of statistical power analysis is thoroughly discussed.*

Lavrakas, P. (1987). *Telephone surveys.* Newbury Park, CA: Sage.

*An important book to read if you are interested in conducting a telephone survey with a sample of people.*

Raj, D. (1972). *The design of sample surveys.* New York: McGraw-Hill.

*This older book discusses the design and sampling issues associated with large surveys.*

Rossi, P. H., Wright, S. D., Fisher, G. A., & Willis, G. (1987). The urban homeless: Estimating composition and size. *Science, 235,* 1336-1341.

*A scholarly article on the difficulties of doing research with the urban homeless.*

Stuart, A. (1984). *The ideas of sampling.* New York: Oxford University Press.

*An interesting addition to a library for the statistically oriented interested in sampling issues.*

Sudman, S. (1976). *Applied sampling.* New York: Academic Press.

*Discusses issues pertaining to the conduct of large surveys and polls.*

# Glossary

**Alpha**   The probability of rejecting the null hypothesis when it is actually true. Tradition keeps the alpha value small—.05, .01, or .001 to avoid rejecting a null hypothesis when it is true (and no difference exists between group means).

**Cluster**   A naturally occurring unit like a school (which has many classrooms, students, and teachers). Other clusters include universities, hospitals, cities, states, and so on. The clusters are randomly selected, and all members of the selected cluster are included in the sample.

**Convenience sample**   A group of individuals who are ready and available.

**Effect size**   Differences between the means $(\mu_1 - \mu_2)$

**Eligibility criteria**   Characteristics of the sample (such as age, knowledge, experience) that render an individual appropriate for inclusion into the survey

**Exclusion criteria**   Characteristics (e.g., too old, live too far away) that rule out certain people from participating in the survey. The survey's findings will not apply to them.

**Focus groups**   Often used in marketing research to find out what a particular component of the public needs and will consume. They usually consist of 10 to 20 people who are brought together to represent a particular population like teens, potential customers, and members of a particular profession.

**Inclusion criteria**   Characteristics of respondents who are eligible for participation in the survey

**Level of significance**   When chosen before the test is performed, is called the alpha value (denoted by the Greek letter $\alpha$)

**Multistage sampling**   Extension of cluster sampling in which clusters are selected and then a sample is drawn from the cluster members by simple random sampling

**Nonprobability sampling**   Some members of the eligible target population have a chance of being chosen for participation in the survey and others do not.

**Null hypothesis** $(H_o)$   Statement that no difference exists between the average or mean scores of two groups

**_p_ value**   Probability that an observed result (or result of a statistical test) is due to chance rather than to participation in a program. It is calculated AFTER the statistical test.

**Probability sampling**   Every member of the target population has a known, nonzero probability of being included in the sample. Probability sampling implies the use of random selection.

**Quota sampling** Population being studied is divided into subgroups, such as male and female and younger and older, and then the proportion of people in each subgroup (e.g., younger and older males and younger and older females) is estimated. The sample is drawn to reflect each proportion.

**Random sampling** Objective means of choosing a sample and is a "fair" way of getting a sample. Members of the target population are selected one at a time and independently. Once they have been selected, they are not eligible for a second chance and are not returned to the pool. Because of this equality of opportunity, random samples are considered relatively unbiased.

**Representative sample** Model of the population. A sample is representative of the population if important characteristics (e.g., age, gender, health status) are distributed similarly in both groups.

**Response rate** Number who respond (numerator) divided by the number of eligible respondents (denominator)

**Sample** Portion or subset of a larger group called a population, which is the universe to be sampled. A good sample is a miniature version of the population.

**Sampling distribution** Means that are computed from a sample. For example, say the mean score in a survey of attitudes toward a bond issue is 50. An examination of an infinite number of means taken from an infinite number of samples would find the means clustering around 50. The means that are computed from each sample form a distribution of values: the sampling distribution. When the sample size reaches 30 or more, the distribution of the sampling means has the shape of the normal distribution.

**Sampling error**   Variation of the sample means around the true value. The sample means tend to gather closer around the true population mean with larger sample sizes and less variation in what is being measured.

**Sampling frame**   List of units that comprise the population from which a sample is to be selected. If the sample is to be representative, then all members of the population must be included on the frame or list.

**Sampling unit**   Individual, group, or other entity that is selected for the survey or assigned to groups

**Snowball sampling**   Type of sampling that relies on previously identified members of a group to identify other members of the population. As newly identified members name others, the sample snowballs in size.

**Standard deviation**   Common measure of dispersion or spread of data about the mean

**Standard error of the mean**   Statistic used to describe the sampling error. The difference between the standard deviation and the standard error of the mean is that the standard deviation tells how much variability can be expected among individuals. The standard error of the mean is the standard deviation of the means in a sampling distribution. It tells how much variability can be expected among means in future samples.

**Stratified random sample**   Population is divided into subgroups or "strata," and a random sample is then selected from each subgroup.

**Systematic sample**   Selecting every nth (5th or 10th or 12th and so on) from a list of eligible survey subjects

**Target population**  Individuals to whom the survey is to apply. You draw a sample from this group of individuals.

**Type I error**  Occurs when differences are found to exist between two groups, although in reality there are no differences. Also called an alpha error.

**Type II error**  Occurs when no differences are found between groups, although in reality there are differences. Also called a beta error.

**Unit of analysis**  Entity whose survey data are examined statistically

# About the Author

ARLENE FINK, PhD, is Professor of Medicine and Public Health at the University of California, Los Angeles. She is on the Policy Advisory Board of UCLA's Robert Wood Johnson Clinical Scholars Program, a health research scientist at the Veterans Administration Medical Center in Sepulveda, California, and president of Arlene Fink Associates. She has conducted evaluations throughout the United States and abroad and has trained thousands of health professionals, social scientists, and educators in program evaluation. Her published works include nearly 100 monographs and articles on evaluation methods and research. She is coauthor of *How to Conduct Surveys* and author of *Evaluation Fundamentals: Guiding Health Programs, Research, and Policy* and *Evaluation for Education and Psychology.*